Mountain Biking For Mere Mortals

by Michael Hodgson

Illustrations by
John McMullen

ICS Books, Inc.
Merrillville, Indiana

Mountain Biking for Mere Mortals

Printed in U.S.A.

DEDICATION

For those of you who would much rather bask in a jacuzzi than pedal up vertical walls and down death-inviting cliffs.

Published by:
ICS Books, Inc.
One Tower Plaza
107 E. 89th Avenue
Merrillville, IN 46410
800-541-7323

Library of Congress Cataloging-in-Publication Data

Hodgson, Michael.
    Mountain biking for mere mortals / by Michael Hodgson.
        p.   cm.
    Includes index.
    ISBN 0–934802–82–3 : $6.99
    1. All terrain cycling.   I. Title.
GV1056.H63 1992   91-40691
796.6--dc20   CIP

Table of Contents

92–39069

iii

PREFACE

In the age of leaping over tall buildings in a single bunny hop (and this while still attached to your toe clips) or grinning famously while riding casually down something most of us would define as a cliff, there comes a need for a book that separates the recommended from the ridiculous.

I personally became enlightened as to the need for such a guide when "invited" to go on a fun ride with several friends not too long ago. The fact that they showed up to the ride with "team scream" fluorescent lycra clinging to huge thigh muscles and reinforced at the knees should have been a tip. Perhaps the fact that they were riding lime green ultra-bright neon duo-tone bikes with the name "Wild Thing" script-painted in pink on the frame should have been another clue. But, no, I grinned foolishly on my rust (real rust mind you, not the fake stuff) and white mountain bike wearing nothing but black lycra shorts, a blue faded t-shirt, an old helmet, and battered gloves. Basically I looked like a Christian naively thanking the Romans for this opportunity to personally feed the lions.

The ride started easily enough, two laps around the parking area. Then, off we zipped, pedaling up and up and up and up and (oh lord) up. Actually, if truth be known, they zipped, I kind of walked, all right, crawled. I'll have you know that it's not easy clinging to the trail with one hand while dragging your bike behind you with the other. One good thing, since my nose was only two inches from the dirt I had little trouble following their tracks. Yep, this sure was fun—hah haa arggg.

When I reached the top, they (my two newly declared enemies for life) were sitting down, casually munching on candy bars and laughing. If I squinted through the mud and sweat-coated haze on my face I could almost detect a speck of dirt and maybe a drop of perspiration on them. Foolishly, I repressed the urge to maim them when they said "Now for the real fun!"

The "real fun," as I was to find out, consisted of a narrow trail winding its way steeply down a virtual rock wall. It's a good thing the two hikers I skidded by were roped together, otherwise I might have scared them right off the rock. I bounced, slid, rolled, and white-knuckled my way back to the car—the last 300 yards without my bike as it got fed up waiting and decided to go on without me.

I was coming to the ignoble realization that perhaps I, despite everything that I truly wanted to believe about myself, was merely mortal and these other fools, who called themselves friends, were mountain biking gods.

Perhaps I should have shown more respect by bowing before their greatness, but that would have to wait until after I backed over them with my car.

 # A Test of Mortality

Before you read on, perhaps you should determine if in fact you are really mortal, or if you have vestiges of mountain bike god lurking somewhere deep in the dark corners of your soul. The following is a carefully designed and worded test to help you come to the right conclusion about your abilities and tendencies. We consulted a panel of experts with the combined IQ of a fully inflated tire, so we know the results will be revealing, if not accurate.

It is important that you get very comfortable before attempting to think about the answers. Have a few sodas, put on some raucous rock and roll, rip open a bag of chips, and flop back on the couch. OK, now carefully read each question and choose the best possible answer that applies to you. In some cases you may find that you will have to exhibit the concentration of a mole, but don't strain yourself—rest if you have to. Are you ready? Begin!

1. Brightly fluorescent lycra makes me feel
   a. like aggressively riding up ridiculously steep mountains and through the valley of death for I shall fear no evil since my mountain bike and tight lycra are with me.
   b. sexy, alluring, and like I should be hanging out on the corner of 6th and Market picking up …never mind.
   c. somewhat nauseous, but since my friends wear it I do too.
   d. like a neon billboard.
2. A helmet is
   a. for moving obstacles out of the way so you can keep riding.
   b. a device designed to ruin all attempts at any decent hairdo other than a plastered one.
   c. a very important safety device to prevent head injuries that would otherwise leave me with the intelligence of a punk rocker or a government official.
   d. a totally hip hat that comes in a variety of colors— although basic black is best because it goes outstandingly well with plaid.
3. Standing at the top of a steep cliff that you have no hope of riding down without killing yourself, you
   a. scream "cowabunga dude" and go for it anyway.
   b. let your bike lead so that you can follow safely several hundred yards behind.
   c. evaluate carefully the consequences of death against the thrill of the ride and walk your bike back the way you came.
   d. pass out.
4. Four close friends all wearing "Team Scream" lycra and riding duo-tone fluorescent bikes invite you along for a fun ride. You
   a. without hesitation tear off the knee brace and head

   bandage (a result of your last fun ride with these
   idiots) and scream "Excellent dudes. Let's go for it!"

   b. would love to, but it is kind of hard to pedal in a full
   body cast so you must decline—maybe next time?

   c. just washed your bike and can't do a thing with it.

   d. feel a sudden need to go to the bathroom to relieve
   yourself for two or three hours.

5. When you think about pain you

   a. begin to salivate hopelessly and immediately
   prepare for your next gnarly ride.

   b. look forward to it as long as it is experienced by
   anyone but you.

   c. wince and complain, but enjoy the attention
   received.

   d. whimper uncontrollably as your spouse puts a
   snoopy bandaid on your boo boo.

6. When faced with a choice between riding through
   an impossibly deep and rocky river or using the
   nearby bridge to cross, you

   a. scream "Truly bodacious dudes, let's have an
   excellent time" as you and your bike disappear
   under water.

   b. think this is really stupid, but if my friends are
   going to try the river I guess I will too.

   c. watch your friends attempt the river crossing,
   laughing uproariously the entire time at their
   near-death experiences, and then casually ride
   across the bridge.

   d. whimper uncontrollably because the bridge is
   too high and the water too deep.

7. Trying to look cool, you lose control of your bike in
   the parking lot. The crash with no apparent obstacles
   in sight happens right at the feet of several gorgeous
   members of the opposite sex whom you have been

dying to impress for years. You

a. get up quickly, do the same thing again and then remark "damn, I just can't get that forward roll with a half twist on my bike down."

b. keep yourself rolling and bouncing for several hundred yards removing trees, other bikers, and several cars in a valiant attempt to solicit sympathy points.

c. look up casually, trying not to look too cool and remark "there I go falling for you again—want to go out before I really hurt myself?"

d. blush, attempt to run away quickly while still attached to your toe clips, and fall flat on your face one more time.

8. You have just hit an unexpected, major drop and a nasty, ugly crash is imminent. As you cartwheel through the air your first thought is for

a. your bike and how can you possibly land so that the bike will fall on top of you thereby protecting the truly excellent neon-duo-tone finish.

b. your bike and how much a new one is going to cost you.

c. your bike and how stupid you were to let your friends talk you into this ride in the first place. Oh, follow that with the realization that once out of hospital you will kill your friends.

d. mommy.

9. You are faced with the ultimate decision—your spouse or your bike. You cannot have both and one or the other will have to go. You decide to

a. keep the bike because it is more fun, doesn't talk back, and is always ready for another ride.

b. keep the bike...no, wait...keep the spouse...no,

wait…the bike, no the spouse—at which point
your spouse leaves with the bike.

c. keep your spouse because you realize that there are
some things that even your bike cannot do.

d. throw a temper tantrum and threaten to hold
your breath until your spouse lets you keep the
bike

10. You always choose a bike ride on the basis of its

a. steep elevation gain, impossible descents,and deep
mud traps capable of swallowing a tank.

b. steep elevation gain, almost impossible descents,
deep mud traps, and a proximity to several 7-11's
with giant sized slurpies.

c. gentle elevation gain, wonderful views, gentle
descents, ending at a spa with mud baths,
massage, and hot tub, and a proximity to a
nearby hospital just in case one of your idiot
friends gets hurt.

d. being paved, level, and only a block or two from
home.

Nice job! Hopefully you are not too drained. Kick
back, have another soda and some more chips. Now for
the moment of truth. Score the results in the following
manner: 4 points for each (a); 3 points for each (b); 2
points for each (c); and 1 point for each (d). Write your
point total here _____. If you scored a perfect 40
you can consider yourself a mountain biking god. This
book is not for you. Put it back on the shelf and pick up
one on The Finer Points of Pain or How To Keep Bugs
From Sticking To Your Teeth On a Truly Bodacious Ride.
If you scored between 30 and 40 points you are floating
somewhere between merely mortal and mountain bike
god. While this book may be too basic for you it should

make entertaining bathroom reading so keep it anyway. If you scored between 15 and 29 points, congratulations! You are merely mortal and this book will become an ideal source of information and little known facts for you. Enjoy the read. Sorry, but if you scored below 15 points you must classify yourself as a nerd and head back to riding with training wheels while wearing plaid. However, if you study really hard and take all the information provided in this book to heart, you do have the hope of someday becoming merely mortal like the rest of us. Good luck!

2 Choosing Your Modus Operandi and Other Complementary Accessories

As a mere mortal, you must come to grips with several very important concepts before charging off to the bike shop to purchase a mountain bike. First, don't worry about performance, you are never going to be a wild enough biker to fully enjoy all the features such as Browning Electronic Accushift Transmissions, Shimano Linear Response and Total Integration Systems, Campagnolo Integrated Global Adjustment Systems, or any other such gadgetry. Resign yourself to what is really important in a mountain bike purchase—do you look good on the bike?

How You Look
Looking good is critically important. It is not how well you can ride, it is how you look that counts. First off, any bike under $500.00 just does not look good and everyone knows it, especially the salesperson. When you ride by on the street, you want people to gape and gasp, not snicker

and chortle. Also, remember that training wheels are not cool at any price.

Technical Jargon

When you are choosing your bike in the store, you must appear to know what you are talking about to get the bike most suitable for your needs. Practice pronouncing the following words and when you can link several phrases together without stumbling, begin using them liberally in casual conversation with the salesperson. They will be very impressed. Are we ready? OK, repeat after the book: saddle (s-a-d-d-l-e), frame (f-r-a-m-e), handlebar (h-a-n-d-l-e-b-a-r), wheels (w-h-e-e-l-s), brakes (b-r-a-k-e-s). Once you have mastered saying these without stuttering, move on to some harder ones: derailleur (day-ray-ler, if you are a Southerner or dee-ray-ler if your preference is Yankee), cotterless crank (mother-in-law), Shimano Deore XT (name-brand-gizmmo-essential-to-sounding-cool). Be cautious of overdoing it and starting to sound like a name dropper.

Sizing Your Bike

Sizing your bike is very important if you ever hope to even get on and ride the thing. First off, straddle the bike. If it feels as if the top tube is somewhere between your navel and your neck and will require surgery to remove it, the bike is a tad too big. Spend a few minutes allowing your voice to stop squeaking before attempting another size run. Ideally, the top tube of the bike should rest two to three inches below the lowest hanging point of your personal anatomy. A good pair of men's lycra shorts will keep this point from being too low and help prevent some men from having to ride a bike with a four inch frame and one inch wheels—great for the ego, but lousy for biking image.

Gear Ratios

Simply put, gear ratio refers to the number of times the rear wheel will turn for every rotation of the chainwheel (the cogged gizmo with pedals). In theory, one can figure gear ratio by dividing the number of teeth on the chainwheel by the number of teeth on the freewheel and then multiplying that by the number of teeth that the snarling doberman will sink into your calf if it catches up with you. If the salesperson asks you about gear ratio, just laugh casually and mention you will adjust it to a 32-24 or 45-13 or 65-30 depending on need or the position of Mars relative to Venus. The salesperson will immediately recognize you as a gear-head and want nothing more to do with you. Of course, you and I both know this was just another successful ploy to cover up the fact that you couldn't change the transmission on your bike if your life depended on it. Anyway, you'll be riding in the lowest gear 100% of the time. The other gears are just for show.

Color Choices

Color is important. You must be careful here. There is a fine line between looking good and an outright misstatement of your riding ability which may cost you dearly in the future. I prefer to stay away from multi-tone duo-iridescent bikes with names like "Wild Thing" stenciled in script down the tubes. Such a bike implies joy in pain, fun in fear, and absolute loathing of anything legal or otherwise ordinary. Mere mortals are not such people nor should we dare to fake it. Stick to single tone, but classy bikes that say "I'm good, but prefer not to show it off."

Accessorizing Your Bike

As far as accessorizing your bike, adhere to the basics. Chrome-metal fenders are definitely not something that should appear on a mountain bike. They give an appearance of nerdism to an otherwise cool attempt at becoming a mountain biker. They also serve to clump up mud between the wheel and fender creating an inopportune jamming of the wheel. This usually results in a spectacular airborn display of a lycra clad rider arcing over the front wheel and into an oncoming tree. Actually, trees should never be considered oncoming since they cannot move, although I must admit there have been times when I would swear that a tree stepped in front of me on purpose.

Kickstand

Kickstands are another accessory that should not find its way onto your bike. Kickstands only serve three purposes: looking stupid; holding your bike up long enough for you to step away before hurling it to the ground;

and dropping into place during a high speed turn. Of course, the good part about the kickstand dropping into place during a high speed turn is the bike will usually remain standing long enough to prevent potential damage to the paint while you recover in the hospital.

Tire Pump

Tire pumps are a good thing as is a tire pressure gauge. Before every ride, check the pressure in your tires. Use the following rough as a guide, the softer the tire the more traction in soft terrain, but the less speed. The harder the tire, the more speed. Since I desire traction above speed I just leave the tires flat and walk my bike, but the choice is yours.

Carrying Strap

The carrying strap every salesperson suggests is not an optional accessory, it is required equipment if you are merely mortal. The strap attaches to the top and seat tubes creating a fairly comfortable carrying surface should the bike ever need to be walked, carried, or burped. In my case, I went with the standard carrying strap and bought optional

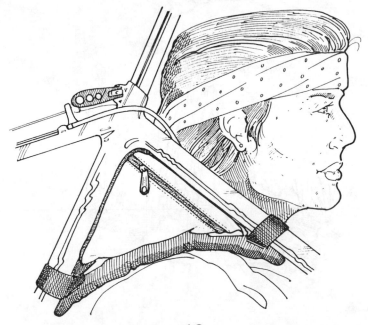

wheels in case I ever needed to ride. Since I seem to spend 99% of my time walking, this was a very good decision.

Water Bottle

A water bottle is essential. How else can you squirt friends in an all-out water fight? Actually, only the water in the water bottle is essential, but since you would have a difficult time carrying water without the bottle, you will need the bottle as well. The water bottle also serves another very important purpose, that of adding several pounds of weight to the bike making it feel more like the three-ton machine you used to ride as a kid. One other important reminder, drink the water if necessary, but don't waste it—you never know when another serious water fight may break out.

Pannier Rack

The mountain bike pannier rack the salesperson will try to sell you is very, very crucial. This rack mounts over the

rear tire and is designed to carry panniers (designer luggage for cyclists) and other assorted gear should you ever want to go touring. Of course, everyone knows that the main reason for the rack is to prevent mud from spraying a dark racing stripe uncoolly up your back. I have discovered one other very critical feature of the rack. Whenever the bike and I are failing to stay in close communion during particularly rocky descents, the rack serves as another resting place for my derriere until such time I am propelled back into the seat— or off the bike which ever comes first.

Toe Clips

Toe Clips are mandatory only because they are ultimately cool. They imply raw power, a go-for-it personality that attacks hills and sneers at anything less than steep. They also lock one's feet to the pedals, which makes for truly spectacular crashes even at slow speeds. There is something impressive about a rider slowly nicking a small rock, weaving for several feet while struggling to get out of the toe clips, and then rolling (sometimes on the bike, sometimes under it) for several more yards—never once losing contact with the pedals. Now that takes skill!

Safety Reflectors

After buying your bike, immediately remove any vestiges of a safety reflector. There is often one on each wheel and sometimes two others, one, just to the front and below the handle bar, and also one to the rear and just below the seat. Sure, safety reflectors are smart to have on your bike when street riding as they warn oncoming cars of your presence at night, but who are we kidding? Your main reason for buying a mountain bike is to look cool, not safe. Leave the reflectors on and everyone knows you really don't ride in the dirt. Take them off and you will leave them guessing—especially in the dark.

14

Bike Calculators

If you plan on toying between the fringes of merely mortal and mountain biking god of wonder, then electronic gadgetry is definitely for you. With a tiny device, no bigger than a Timex watch, you can time your ride, calculate distances ridden, determine altitude, eliminate unidentified riders, jam police radar, and control a robot that serves to convince your spouse you are home cleaning the garage instead of enjoying yourself.

Roof Racks

Bike roof racks are only important as status symbols. No one actually uses them since a serious injury could result from trying to lift and balance a 30 pound object 10 feet over one's head while attempting to secure it to the roof rack with your teeth. It is true that many people drive around town in BMW's and SAAB's with bikes safely on top of their roof racks, but in fact these people just bought the vehicles with the bikes already installed from previous car owners who couldn't figure out how to get the bikes off without killing themselves.

Dressing for Success

You may have heard the phrase "dress for success." Well, mountain bike riding is no different. Some people insist on dressing like a racer, fully logoed and draped in fluorescence. Even if you can barely pedal out of your driveway without weaving, dressing like a riding god implies suave and skill. Looking good without actually being good can be risky though. If someone really good asks you to go for a ride, your only alternative is an extended trip to the bathroom—it's either that or get laughed out of town.

Personally, I recommend dressing somewhere between nerd and god. That way you safely leave perceptions about

nerd and god. That way you safely leave perceptions about potential skill level to the imagination. Stick to solid colors such as cobalt, royal, or black. Fuchsia, yellow, and peach will draw unnecessary attention to yourself and present a real danger to your personal well-being anywhere within a fifty mile radius of a truck stop.

Riding Shorts

Riding shorts that look as though they were spray painted on that morning are an absolute necessity.

are widely acknowledged to prevent chaffing, increase riding comfort, and cure all manner of worldly ills. A little known, but equally important feature is that the shorts will double as a sling shot should you ever get lost and have to hunt for food to survive.

One word of caution regarding lycra riding shorts. Because of their very revealing design, lying about one's religious affiliation or sexual endowment is a virtual impossibility. Remember, lycra takes the phrase "I have nothing to hide" to an all new level.

Mountain Biking Jersey

The mountain biking jersey is no different than a road cycling jersey. It bonds to the skin, looks ridiculous, and loudly advertises the manufacturer's name—for what reason I cannot fathom. I sure wouldn't want my name on something that looks like a bowling shirt with fanny pockets. Should you wonder why such a stupid and expensive shirt is so popular, try this little trick. Take a plastic garbage bag (make sure it is skin tight after you cut neck and arm holes), glue your name to the back in reflective letters, attach colorful streamers to the sides, and win several major bicycling events. Then sit back and watch all the manufacturers hustle to create the skin-tight-reflective-garbage-bag-jersey you wore and pay you millions for it—get the idea?

Riding Shoes

Riding shoes are more than just stiff tennis shoes. They are stiff tennis shoes with an attitude that cost three times the price of a normal shoe. This price reflects the hours of testing, the hiring of a blind color-coordinating expert, and the influence of a neon-crazed fashion designer. Of course, one must realize that a cyclist's riding ability is directly proportional to the price of the shoes divided by the cost of the bicycle multiplied by the number of riders wearing team jerseys.

Riding Gloves

If you are in the market for a unique fashion statement, then riding gloves are a must. The nifty little oval tan on the back of an otherwise white hand is a superb conversation piece and makes a great point of reference when comparing tan lines. The gloves are fingerless, which means that you get to pay more for less. They are also padded in the palm. The padding is to insure hand protection while desperately grabbing passing trees as you flash downhill at 700 mph on the "casual" ride that has just burned up what was left of your brake pads.

Cycling Cap

The cyclist's painters cap is a remarkable garment. What other sport offers the participant an opportunity to purchase a completely useless article of clothing for more than the price of a good t-shirt? Why cyclists began wearing the hats is a mystery in the first place. Why cyclists continue to insist upon wearing them is beyond ordinary comprehension. However, the fact still remains; if you want to be admitted to the name-brand cycling clubs, be accepted by the beautiful people, and generally be recognized as something worth conversing with—wear the silly thing.

Helmet

The helmet is a very useful head protection device designed to be the only item, other than your head which is in the helmet, that survives a wicked crash without falling apart. Fools that ride without a helmet are often referred to affectionately as organ donors by appreciative emergency room doctors and nurses. Helmets are also the chief reason cycling cap sales are so high. After a day in a helmet, there is nothing left to do with plastered hair other than hide it discreetly under a stupid cycling cap.

Sunglasses

Don't even think of riding anywhere without a pair of sunglasses that give everyone the impression that you are an honorary crew-member of the Starship Enterprise. Aside from the seemingly minor benefit of providing sufficient protection from the sun so that you can see, a good pair of sunglasses offer wind and bug protection.

3 Riding Techniques to Help You Avoid Near Death and Other Such Unpleasantries

It is customarily acknowledged that in order to be acceptably proficient at anything, one must practice. Failing this, one must master the art of deception. On a positive note, since monkeys, bears, and even dogs ride bicycles it is apparently a fairly easy sport to master—ha ha ha arggg crash!

Warming Up

Before attempting any riding, face planting, or tree pruning you need to be quite limber. Your body should have the characteristics of Gumby when properly limbered, and snap back into place no matter how hard the impact. However, if during stretching exercises you find yourself oozing into small cracks and crevices, abort! You are too limber and in danger of becoming slime mold, destined to spend the rest of your life clinging to trees.

The appropriate stretching regimen should consist of

toe touches, leg lifts, hurdlers, and grass pickers following a well balanced breakfast. In a pinch, consume one dozen chocolate frosted donuts and several mugs of jet-black coffee in rapid succession. Follow this with a brisk warm-up walk to the nearest restroom and a final swig of coffee.

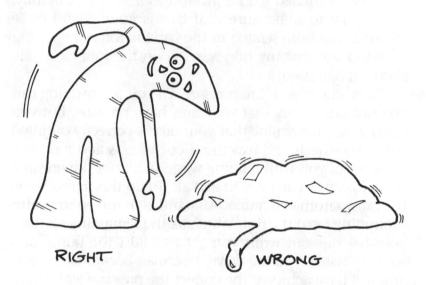

RIGHT   WRONG

Safety Check

The safety check is designed to help you identify potential mechanical problems that could cause discomfort or inconvenience when on the ride. For example: you begin riding, but feel your seat is far more uncomfortable than normal. Not wanting the others to think you are a whimp you keep riding, trying to ignore the searing pain radiating out from your posterior. At lunch, unable to sit down or walk normally, you ask a friend to help you adjust your seat;

at which point your friend exclaims "what seat?" Now, had you performed the patented safety check at the outset, you would have noticed that your bike was missing its seat and that the potential for discomfort from the exposed seat post was high.

Immediately after getting out of the car and having your bike winched to the ground look it over carefully. Check first to make sure that this is your bike. I once rebuilt a bike from scratch in the parking lot, not realizing until too late that my ride was still on the roof rack. Talk about embarrassed!

Next, check your tire pressure. Of course, by doing this you not only verify that your tires have pressure, but you conclusively determine that your bike is correctly outfitted with two wheels and two tires (four wheels and four tires for those of you with training wheels). If your tire pressure is too low, you will need to add air. To do this, remove the tire pump from the frame. Attach the pump to the valve protruding from the rim. Watch all the remaining air from your tire hiss out while you try to adjust the pump and securely fasten it to the valve. Pump air back into the tire. You will have achieved the correct tire pressure after about two to three hours at which point you will be too fatigued to ride and opt to wait for the others to come back. Be sure that you over-inflate your tires by two to three hundred pounds as this will compensate for all the air that rushes out when you disconnect the pump from the valve.

Step three, visually inspect your bike. Look for missing spokes, missing seat, missing handlebars, missing frame. If any parts are missing, distract your friend and borrow his. Of course, he will immediately notice that something is missing from his bike and employ the same borrowing technique from you. As this will go back and forth for several hours before anyone catches on, it is highly recommended that you either pack spare parts or a spare bike. Otherwise, you will spend all your time in the parking lot wandering around in a confused manner.

Finally look over the drive train of the bike and your brake system. There should be lots of grease, a chain, some wires, various cogs and cranks, and the rear wheel should spin when the pedals are rotated in a forward manner. The brakes should provide enough friction to stop the wheels from spinning when the levers (the ones on the handlebars) are squeezed. If not, either adjust the brakes, borrow your friend's bike, or resort to jamming your boot into the wheel every time you need to stop.

Getting On

While this may seem simple enough, there are several techniques that must be discussed for your convenience and survival. First is the parking lot mount. This is

accomplished by first inserting your left foot in the left pedal while it is in the down position (the pedal, not your foot). Next, after pushing off with your right foot to gain momentum, casually swing your right leg over the seat, sit down, and then fumble for two to three minutes while trying to get your right foot in the pedal and toe clip. Once the foot is securely in the pedal, look up in time to see the oncoming tree which is conveniently there to slow your momentum while you wait for your friends. Resume pedaling immediately after disengaging yourself from the branches.

The second technique is the uphill mount. This is only slightly more difficult. Mountain biking trails and their accompanying guide books have been carefully designed to provide momentum-stopping confusion at the bottom of every steep hill. Of course, you won't realize it is a steep hill until you get off your bike to look at the map and determine that the way you must go heads straight up while the easy trails go nowhere. First, insert your left foot in the left pedal. Now, push off violently with your right foot and swing it desperately over the saddle. You should now be uselessly fumbling for the other pedal while your bike wavers to a stop. At the last moment before impact, you should give up trying to get your right foot in the toe clip and just pedal, with the pedal upside down and the toe clip dragging in the dirt. Good! Your face should be red, your eyes bugging out, and your bike should be climbing the hill at the rate of two to three feet per hour. You will make the top in several days unless you lose momentum.

The third technique is the downhill mount. Steep downhills always occur after lunch or a long rest break. This is designed so you will have plenty of opportunity to think about death and what a great idea it was to go on this ride. First, point the front tire downhill. Squeeze the brakes with your hands to hold the bike steady while you place your left foot in the left toe clip. Next, as you release the brakes, swing your right foot over the seat. At this point you should be reaching Mach 1. By the time you get somewhat seated (either on the seat, the pannier rack, or the handle bars) you will be at Mach 2 and the G forces will make it virtually impossible to find the other pedal, but keep trying. You can be happy in the knowledge that your friends are finding this most hilarious. By the time you reach Mach 3 and the smell of burning rubber begins filling your nostrils, you will separate from your bike resulting in an immediate deceleration of your person. Not to worry, all this is perfectly normal. After reattaching all the missing body parts—yours, not the bikes—finish

walking down the final few feet and mount your bike as described for the parking lot mount.

Perhaps this may seem silly mentioning at this point, but you do know you are supposed to face the handlebars, don't you?

Around the Parking Lot

It is important that you perform the perfunctory several laps around the parking lot. Why is it important? No one really knows, but everyone does it so go with the flow. Be sure to gaze intently down at your drive chain, your brakes, and then shift through your gears several times to assure yourself that they are really there. Glance up in time to get a good look at the oncoming parked car before swerving into the bushes. This last technique is called a practice fall and is essential in determining if you are truly ready and able to reattach body parts before the critical point in a ride—the start.

Using Your Eyes

Squeezing your eyes shut as you career downhill towards an awaiting log is not considered good technique. How can you fully enjoy the fear if you aren't able to accurately observe the speed and inevitability of an oncoming impact?

Use the sidewinder glance when passing a cluster of gorgeous members of the opposite sex clad in revealing lycra. Correct technique involves somewhat of a downward and sideways glance, giving the appearance of reading the trail and surrounding terrain. Properly executed, no one will realize what has just occurred, especially if you are wearing sunglasses to contain the eyes popping out of your sockets. Improperly executed, you are liable to suffer the direct glare and sidewinder uppercut from your spouse.

Anytime that you pass anyone riding a bike in the same direction as you, either uphill or down, it is important to sneer appropriately. Rolling your eyes and laughing derisively shows utter contempt for this other feeble-bodied individual attempting to enjoy him or herself on the ride. Rolling your eyes and laughing derisively also serves to cover up the excruciating pain you are now feeling because your competitive spirit has once again convinced your body to try something for which it was never intended—raw physical exertion.

Never become preoccupied with an obstacle ahead of you. Constant staring at a stump near the trail will only result in the stump moving into the trail to greet you and you leaving the trail and your bike behind in a wonderful show of aerial acrobatics.

Shifting Gears

Your bike has been blessed with between 18 and 21 possible gear choices. The idea behind all these gear choices is to utterly confuse you, resulting in thigh-slapping good times for your friends as they observe you either slip a gear on a downhill transition and introduce your vitals to the top-tube, or selecting too high a gear on an uphill and explode under the pressure of trying to pedal in a gear even Rambo couldn't push. Save yourself all the trouble. Leave your gear in the lowest possible selection at all times. The other gears are intended for show and you will just wear them out faster if you use them anyway.

Creek Crossings

Creek crossings will weed out the merely mortal from the mountain biking gods every time. Merely mortal riders wet their pants before the crossing while gods get their pants wet during the crossing. Either way, you've got wet pants. The idea is to maintain enough momentum through the running water so that you don't get hung up and go for an unplanned swim. Remember at all times that no matter what, this is fun. So what if you have just completed the inevitable endo and face-planted yourself in the stream. So what if your bike is floating down to who knows where. So what if you are wet and cold. The important thing to remember is your friends are laughing up a storm and you have provided them with this unequaled opportunity to enjoy themselves. So what if you want to kill them. Relax and revel in their good humor. You can always dismantle their bikes with a chainsaw later.

Log Jumping

No, this is not a section about logs jumping out of your way to ensure an unobstructed path to biking nirvana, although that would be special. Instead, picture yourself on a nice gentle downhill, not too much speed. The trail is tranquil and smooth, sunlight trickles through the leaves, dancing on the earth beneath. Suddenly, a rogue log appears out of nowhere in front of you. There is no alternative, you cannot ride around it so you must go over. In theory, you yank up on your front wheel, performing what is known in technical bike jargon as a wheelie. As the front wheel lands on the other side of the log you pedal firmly forward and the rear wheel follows.

In reality, you will attempt the front wheel lift, maybe even getting the front wheel over the log successfully. Just as the words "alright dude" are leaping out of your lips, the rear wheel bounces into the log causing the seat to jump up and smack you in the posterior end, causing you to become another statistic arching gracefully over the front handlebars and impacting firmly into a wayward bush or tree.

Another possibility is that you will get the front wheel over the log, but come to an immediate stop as the back wheel successfully absorbs every ounce of the bike's forward momentum. However, your forward momentum is still in high gear, ejecting you out of the seat. Fortunately, your crotch will manage to slow your forward momentum by impacting with the bike's headset, giving you an opportunity to slide gracefully off the bike and take two to three hours to remember how to breathe.

Of course, if by some miracle of miracles you do successfully negotiate the log, you will end up looking over your shoulder at the log causing you to lose control and crash into an oncoming tree. Either way, over or not, the sight isn't pretty. Why fellow mortals don't follow my lead and get off their bikes to walk them over the obstacle is unbelievable. Live and learn.

Climbing Hills

There is a fine line between actually pedaling up a hill and walking or crawling up. I am an expert in crawling. Realizing early on that I was destined to either lean so far forward that my rear tire would spin hopelessly, or so far back that my front tire went orbital, I learned the art of bike crawling.

To properly initiate the bike crawl, you must first attempt to pedal up the hill. With your eyes bugging out, your breathing rhythm similar to that of an angry bull, and your hands clenched desperately to the handlebar grips, you grind tenuously up the first several feet. Then, your bike begins to succumb to negative momentum. It leans, and, ever so slowly as if to imply the wait is almost more painful than the final impact, you fall. At this point, getting up is more trouble than it's worth.

Save time and effort by first removing your feet from the toe clips. Then, carefully remove any impaled objects from your person. Finally, grunting and moaning loudly for sympathetic effect, begin scrambling on hands and knees, dragging your bike bravely behind you as if nothing can stop your iron-willed desire to reach the top. In reality, all you are doing is trying to get out of the way of a herd of idiots actually trying to pedal up behind you.

For those of you still inclined to attempt pedaling up the hills because it seems easier, consider this: why kill yourself pedaling when everyone else is walking and getting there just as fast as you with half the effort?

Descending Hills

You really have three choices: walk; ride as long as your brakes hold out; close your eyes and pray. In the last case, refer to sections on power stopping and power panicking for additional information. If you choose not to walk, fool that thou are, you will need to keep the following in mind. Ride slowly and apply heavy brake action. Avoid using too much front brake unless you find joy in a forward wheelie followed by a useful deceleration method, the lip stop. If the brakes begin to smoke, begin to pray. If the brakes wear out, your speed will increase geometrically (refer to the power stopping and power panicking techniques listed below).

Sudden Drop-Offs

Experts will tell you never to ride blindly off a sudden drop. Thank you very much for that advice. I feel, if a drop-off is sudden, how is one supposed to know until it happens? Theory has it that if you watch your speed, you should be able to detect a sudden drop well in advance, but who are we kidding here? In reality, what the experts mean is never ride blindly off a sudden drop a second time, providing you survive the first. Now, that makes good sense.

Cornering

Cornering is the technique used to successfully get you and your bike around a bend in the trail at anything faster than a walk. The optimum goal is to get around the corner at the same time, however this is not mandatory as long as sometime after the corner you and your bike reunite and continue with the forward momentum.

Power Turning

Power turning is an advanced form of cornering at an unusually high rate of speed, usually during an unanticipated downhill and just before a full-on power panic. This technique is not to be used frequently as it is hard on the nerves. Use caution as there is always a fine line between a successful power turn and power stop—see below. A power turn occurs when, as trees, bushes, and your life are beginning to flash by during a "fun" downhill, you realize that the trail bends left or right to avoid a big tree or rock. Your arms begin to lock and your gaze fixates on the impending painful impact. At the last moment, your mind will override the instinct to panic and lean desperately in the direction of the turn. If all goes well, your body will follow your mind and the bike will follow shortly thereafter, whizzing around the turn and scraping paint off on the obstacle. You now have permission to laugh derisively at death. However, if your body forgets to follow your mind and you continue straight into the obstacle, not to worry. You have just effected a picture perfect power stop and can skip over the next section.

Power Stopping

Power stopping is one of the easier skills to master. First you must achieve a very high rate of speed. Next, with your eyes tearing from the wind rushing by, find the nearest gopher hole, log, large rock, or stray tree. The immediate deceleration experienced is normal as is the flashing of white lights and stars. To be effective, the power stop should bring both you and your bike to a 0 mph position within several feet of initiation. If you lost contact with your bike for any reason, your technique has not been perfected and you should practice often until such time both you and your bike can complete the 60—0 mph stop in unison. Be careful not to damage the environment or the trees. It is best, while your technique is still rusty, to practice on brick walls and in parking garages. Of course, if you have any hope of living a long and prosperous life, you will learn to use your brakes instead of solid objects.

Power Panicking

Power panicking is a very important skill to retain, especially during a particularly steep downhill. Learning not to fight the primal urges to run, pull hair, and scream in the face of imminent doom is an acquired skill. To appropriately effect the delivery of a power panic, one must remember several key points. First, you must master the look of sheer terror on your face. The eyes must be wide open and searching for something your hands can grab in a vain attempt to slow the downhill momentum. The mouth is to be kept gaping at all times with a scream half-way out and frozen on the vocal cords. Your skin must take on the glow of white ash.

Next, your hands must be locked in a death grip, clutching the handlebars as if your life depended on it— which of course you know it does. Forget about a relaxed grip and supple arms. You are trying to attempt the difficult full-on power-panic and no amount of proper technique-induced coaching should ever get in the way.

Remember to lock the knees, the back should be rigid, and your face should have the appearance of being frozen with

jaws agape in horror. Breathing is strictly optional at this point.

Finally, with the front wheel bouncing and careening off things and the back wheel sliding and skidding, you crash. Not just any crash, but a spectacular barrel roll, half gainer, with a forward twist crash. Your friends will stand in awe and applaud any sign of life, Remember to weakly wave your hand to the crowd, stagger to your feet, and get back on your bike for the final several feet of hill. Be sure you are facing the correct way first. I once had a friend ride back up the hill he just rode down before realizing his mistake. The emotional breakdown was really unbecoming.

One Hand Riding

Experts love this drill. They actually recommend using one hand in a level area when learning to use your body, and not the handlebars to turn the bike. While this may work for expert riders who are used to staying in one location such as the seat for an entire ride, it doesn't work for those of us who are all over the bike and then some. Just last week on a relatively calm downhill I migrated from the seat to the pannier rack to the top tube to hanging over the handlebars and then back to the seat; no easy task let me tell you. I even had several agents ask me if I took my act on the road. To imagine myself doing all that without both hands on the handlebars is not only terrifying, it is impossible.

Riding Backwards

Although this is a somewhat rare occurrence, it is worth mentioning. I have seen people riding backward because they got on the bike incorrectly. Remember, the handlebars are at the front of the bike and intended to be held with your hands. Refer back to the section about getting on a bike if you have any questions. I have also seen people actually riding down a hill, backwards. Perhaps they lost momentum and brakes on an uphill and the only alternative was to coast back down. Who knows? If this should happen to you, the best solution is to effect a power stop. Refer to the section above.

What To Do When Your Bike Ends Up Riding You

Strictly speaking, this should never happen, even in the best of circles. If you do find yourself in the embarrassing position of having your bike ride you, it is best to lay low for a while and let the whole thing blow over. I mean really, if God had intended that to happen he would have given you a saddle and wheels and the bike . . .well never mind.

Getting Off

Ideally, you and the bike should come to a complete and gradual stop together. Before coming to a complete stop, casually remove one foot from the toe clip, lean in that direction and rest your weight on your free foot. Casually swing your other leg over the saddle leaving both feet firmly planted on the ground next to your bike. I have seen some people attempt to lean in the direction of the foot still in the toe clip, but this only results in an embarrassingly slow fall, usually at the feet of someone you are trying to impress.

There are always exceptions to tradition and some situations involving a dismount are less than ideal although the final outcome remains the same. These rare and whimsical dismounts, guaranteed to provide you and your family with a lifetime of nifty memories, may result in you and your bike coming to a complete stop at separate times and places. There is really no way to practice this type of dismount, but you will know without a doubt when it occurs. Get used to these impromptu occurrences, but try not to get carried away with them.

Stationary Balancing

You've seen this performed at circuses and city intersections across the country. A cyclist comes to a red light or some other momentum halting device and stays upright with his feet still in the pedals. How is this possible? Don't kid yourself, they are not doing this intentionally. Most riders who are seen performing this hazardous trick are actually stuck to their pedals and dealing emotionally with the very real possibility they are destined to spend the rest of their lives attached to their bikes.

According to legend, the biker who first invented this technique was none other than Mr. Uni, inventor of the Unicycle. While temporarily stuck to his pedals one day, he discovered that by turning his front wheel slightly on a subtle grade, maintaining constant, but gentle pressure with his pedals, and letting gravity work with him, he could remain upright for several seconds. Through much effort and a certain amount of trial and error, Mr. Uni found it was easier to balance on one wheel, thereby creating the unicycle. Other cyclists seem to be skeptical however, and continue to practice this inadvisable technique in public, creating traffic jams and in some instances convincing other riders to try it too. Don't buy into this insidious Communist trick.

Road Riding

Reality is sometimes hard to swallow. Get used to it. It is vital that you come to grips with the fact that 90% of your riding is going to be on paved roads. Don't panic, as long as you have carefully followed all of my equipment and dressing suggestions in the preceding chapters, no one will suspect otherwise, to them you are a mountain biker. However, since much of your

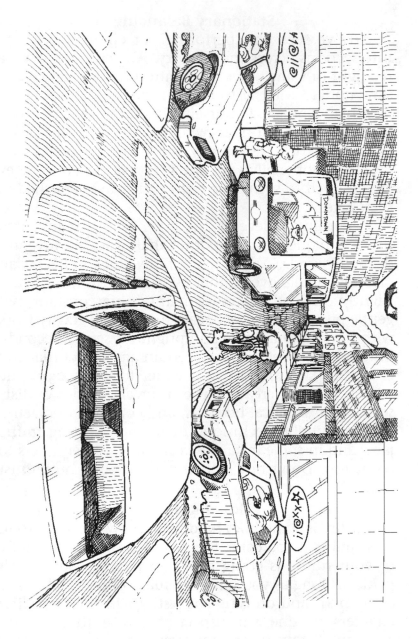

riding will be done secretly on the streets, it is important that you grasp some basic road riding skills necessary to survive. Try not to draw undue attention to yourself.

It is true that most street accidents result from biker error. For example, not correctly identifying the difference between the express and commuter bus can be the difference between a safe turn and becoming something they have to scrape off the grill later. Everyone knows express busses (and taxis too) yield for nothing and have every legal right to swerve in and out of traffic in an attempt to hit pedestrians and bikers. Learn this and your life will become much more predictable.

Predictable is something that a biker needs to be to stay alive in the big city. Always weave in and out of parked cars, run red lights, ride in the opposite direction of traffic, and never use hand signals. Of course this is dangerous and only fools would ride this way, that's the point. Since everyone else does it, you should too. Riding safely and obeying all laws will only startle drivers and pedestrians which could result in a serious accident involving you. Be predictable, ride dangerously like everyone else.

Stay alert. This is so critical that it bears repeating, stay alert. That car you cut off earlier may try to open its car door on you. That pedestrian you swore at just a moment ago may turn out to be the same person that repairs your bike later in the week—not a good omen. You must remain alert at all times to potential hazards and pitfalls. Speaking of pitfalls, always avoid open manholes. Even though that nut from Cheers (Woody is it?) has been seen in a less-than-intelligent beer commercial riding through sewers and popping up from manholes in an attempt to win the Tour De Lite, common sense tells me that this is not good practice.

Etiquette and Style For the Well Groomed and Educated Rider

Although there will be very few of you actually riding your bikes on the dirt, this section is important. Should you ever venture out of your driveway with your bike, you will need to understand some basic rules of etiquette if you are to remain respectable and prevent slipping to the depths of a lycra-clad, neon-crazed, multi-gearheaded fiend.

Written Rules of the Trail

1. Always ride safely and in control—safety first. What this really means is you should stay safely in the parking lot while your other friends attempt to kill themselves on the ride. You can view yourself as the designated driver, the only person with enough working body parts after the ride to be able to operate the car's clutch and steering wheel at the same time.

2. Ride carefully and obey the rules of the road. Since there is no road, there can be no rules, a major failing in mountain bike etiquette in my humble opinion.

3. Maintain a speed that is easily controlled at all times and is safe for you and others. This is viewed in terms of Mach speeds by mountain bike gods. If you are at least a blur, you can be avoided, if you can't be seen then you are not there, and if you are clearly in view the rider must be walking. Any normal person would recognize this as unsafe! I was once caught up in the draft of a passing rider going Mach 3 for over 5 days before landing somewhere near Cleveland.

4. Yield the right-of-way to other trail users. This is easy, rather like the old game paper-scissors-rock. Equestrians kick hikers and bikers. Hikers kick bikers. Bikers are slime. Of course, you and I know this is not true, but try telling that to a 1000 pound stallion and a mob of angry hikers with hiking staffs.

5. Stay out of the wilderness areas and all other places closed to mountain bikes. Officially, this means that anywhere easy and safe to ride is off limits. Areas like Harlem, the LA Barrios, Half Dome in Yosemite (the steep side), the Gobi Desert, the Eiger, and the valley

of death are permissible. Remember to ride carefully or bikers may be declared off limits in these areas too.

6. Respect livestock and wildlife. Personally, if a large Bovine, or something else that can squash me and my bike with a look is standing in the middle of the trail, it's got my complete respect and attention.

7. Do not litter. For mountain bikers, this means nothing more than picking up all stray parts after a spectacular downhill. Hikers do not take kindly to coming across dentures, fingernails, bits of broken frame, cracked helmets, or pieces of torn lycra littering their trail. Show respect for the land and carry out everything that was attached when it went in.

8. Be prepared. To be adequately prepared means you are able to deal with any emergency as it arises. Death is considered an emergency, as is fear and panic. In order for you to be truly prepared to handle these and other emergencies there are some essential items that you should carry with you at all times. They are in random order: a tire repair kit; water; extra snacks; a mini-tool kit; spare spokes; spare bike; and spare friends. A priest, an emesis bag, a paper bag to hyperventilate in, and tissues to blow your nose are extra weight but worth considering if you are planning on attempting a particularly terrifying ride.

Ask Mr. Humble, Letters on Style and Etiquette

Dear Humble:

I have heard that if I am riding along a trail and encounter a group of horses, I should get off my bike and let

them by. This doesn't seem fair. Don't bikers have rightstoo?
  Questioning life in Petaluma

Dear Pet:

  Though this may not seem fair, consider the alternatives. While riding by a cluster of horses one of them may decide to sit on you. There is also a recent scientific study that has determined lycra-clad riders on neon bikes are attractive to certain stallions. Now, I don't know about you, but personally the idea of a 3000 pound stallion getting star-struck over me on a bike is less than appealing. Do yourself a favor, walk and stop worrying about fair. By the way, that's Mr. Humble to you.

Dear Mr. Humple:

Every week I go riding with the same group of friends. There is this one girl that I really like, but she doesn't seem to know I am alive. How can I get her attention.

Dateless in Detroit

Dear Date:

You want her to notice you in clammy lycra while wearing a helmet that authentically recreates ancient Roman hairstyles? Get a real life or wear a suit next time. By the way, that's Mr. Humble, not Humple.

Dear Mr. Humble:

One of the women in our riding group insists on wearing lycra, despite the fact that she is, well, decidedly large and heavy. We enjoy her company, she has a great personality, but get nauseated anytime her lycra-clad wide-body comes into view. What should we do?

Slim in Jacksonville

Dear Slim:

This is a free country Slim, and unfortunately anyone, I mean anyone can wear lycra. However, for the record, your decidedly plump friend (and any other cellulite clad individual, male or female) should be aware that she is endangering the lives of everyone she loves by insisting on wearing lycra. Lycra was never designed to be worn by those individuals that stretch it to its load limit repeatedly. It has been reported that if just one lycra stretch pant worn by an individual that is 100 pounds overweight lets go, the rapid release of cellulite could destroy anything standing or riding within 10 feet of the explosion. My advice to you if she continues to wear lycra, is to establish a "safe zone" of fifty feet around her at all times. You are a very brave man, keep us posted.

Dear Mr. Humble:

I've been doing a lot of riding in the Pacific Northwest and my glasses keep fogging up. I've heard that spitting on your glasses will help alleviate the problem, but isn't it bad manners to spit in public. That's what mommy used to say.

Drooling in Seattle

Dear Drool:

Yes, spitting is a public offense and liable to get you two to three minutes detention. However, it does help to prevent your glasses from fogging. Of course, there is a problem with this method. If you are one of those people who does not practice acceptable oral hygiene techniques such as brushing at least once a week, you run the risk of creating a burning sensation in your eyes and an eventual loss of vision due to heavy tearing. Hope this helps and remember, only fools spit into the wind when they are riding.

Environmental Impact of a Face Plant

Let's face it (pun intended). Any crash or loss of control by you, the bike rider, results in a distinctive gouge or smear

on the surface of whatever you come in violent contact with, tree, rock, or ground. In the interests of preserving the environment for our children, and to leave the area as good, if not better than when you visited, it is critical that you learn to select appropriate crash sites that will not result in permanent, irreparable damage to the ecological well being of the area you are riding in. If such a site is not immediately available, attempt to stay airborn long enough to find a more suitable location. The future of our environment depends on it.

Is Lycra a Responsible Ecological Statement?

Actually, no. Lycra is a petroleum based product (which accounts for its amazing ability to slide off any seat known to man) that was invented by Lycram Hussein, a direct descendent of the present owner of Iraq. This man brilliantly realized that as more and more Americans were beginning to conserve and drive fuel-efficient cars, oil would become less valuable. Capitalizing on American vanity, the biking boom, and Hollywood, Lycram came up with a substance that would stretch to unbelievable limits and would revolutionize the fashion world, thus ensuring a higher price for oil and security for the Middle East. Contrary to popular opinion, lycra is not a third world plot to embarrass overweight Americans. It is however, the reason Iraq invaded Kuwait and why the allied forces invaded the Middle East—to defend freedom and America's addiction to tight clothing.

5

Caring For Your Steed and Basic Maintenance Tips That Can Be Performed With A Mallet

Cleaning Your Bike

As you stand there before your formerly brand new mountain bike, you may be wondering "How did it ever get so dirty, and where did those scratches come from, and why is there oil and grease gunked all over the chain, and why can't I keep my bike looking like a professional's bicycle?" The answer is of course obviously simple; professionals never put themselves in a situation where they will actually have to clean a bike. Bike reviewers and other bike magazine professionals don't take their bikes out of the studio. Yes, that's right, the images of dirt, steep hills, and nasty terrain are all superimposed on the negative after the picture of the bike professional on a shiny new bike has been taken in the studio. Everyone knows that if the shot were actually attempted outdoors, the bike would become too dirty and scratched to be usable for anything but selling to ordinary folk like you and me.

How do mountain bike racers keep their bikes so clean? Again, they don't. After a particularly grueling race pounding down rocky slopes, across muddy rivers, and up sandy washes, the bike racer hands his bike to the bike mechanic who takes one disgusted look, says "YECHHH!" and throws the entire bike out. How can the racer afford that? He can't, but the bike sponsor who is supplying him with brand new bikes can. Remember, the bike pro gets paid to look good.

Cleaning Yourself

No matter what you do, or how careful you are, you are going to get dirty while mountain biking. Hundreds of thousands of mountain bikers seek counseling every year when the healthy tan they thought they were acquiring washes off in the shower to reveal a phosphorescent white luster. Pig Pen, of Charlie Brown fame, was a prototype mountain biker. Expect a sneer and a look of gross contempt upon returning home from a particularly enjoyable, but muddy ride. Also expect to be tossed the dog's wash tub, a towel, a car scrub brush, and a hose with the jet attachment. Your spouse is informing you that you have clogged up the tub with mud and grease for the last time and from now on you shower with the dogs.

Lubricating and Massaging Your Bike

Mountain bikes are a finicky lot. After several weeks of riding, they will begin to whine, squeak, groan, and grunt, rather like a husband after an intense afternoon of softball and beer or a wife after the annual Mervyn's sale. If you and your bike are to continue with your harmonious relationship, you must listen to all of the bike's complaints attentively and tend to each one fervently. Apply oil to everything that moves, polish to every square inch of paint and chrome, grease the saddle, and kneel before your bike reciting mantra s. If this special treatment fails to work, smack your bike over the headset with a mallet or iron skillet, that should get its attention.

Tools You Will Need Other Than a Mallet

Wrenches: Carry a complete set. Of course, no matter how complete your set, the size needed is always back on your workbench.

Crow-bar: This is to extract your bike from particularly nasty areas after particularly ugly crashes (optional).

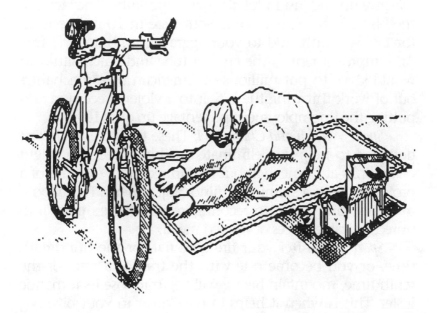

KY Jelly; This is to extract the seat from particularly nasty areas after an extremely bumpy ride (optional).

Hammer: Perfect for those emergency repairs like realigning the front forks of your bike after an unseen pothole and for beating back 300 pound dogs named Killer with an appetite for aluminum alloy or raw meat on the pedal (optional).

Tire Irons and Tire Repair Kit: The tire irons are tools that will allow you to remove your tire from the wheel while hopelessly nicking, bending, and scratching your rim beyond reasonable repair. Tire irons were designed by rim manufacturers to ensure a steady stream of customers. The tire repair kit is nothing more than a very toxic glue and a selection of patches so that you can "field" repair any punctures and leaks.

Spare Tube: You will carry this because inevitably, after several hours trying to repair the 30th leak in your tire you will give up and just install the new inner-tube. The fact that the bike mechanic will repair your tube in 10 milliseconds for $25 will only add to your aggravation, but don't fret. Any improvement in the current tube and patch situation would serve to put millions of American bike mechanics out of work throwing the U.S. into a violent recession and putting the unemployment percentage up over 10%.

Spoke Wrench and Chain Tool: These tools are, in theory, designed to help you eliminate wobbly wheels and tight chain links at home, without the unnecessary expense of a professional for a seemingly minor adjustment. These tools, in reality, only serve to reconfigure your bike's parts into unrecognizable peices of warped metal.

Spare Car: After your tire goes flat for the hundredth time, or you become one with the trail or a tree for the tenth time, mountain biking will begin to lose its romantic luster. This is when it helps to have a car in your bike bag that you can just pull out and drive away in (optional).

Dealing With Noises Like "Sproing" and "Shnickity-Shnickity"

Noises are a bike's way of talking to you, or in certain special cases of laughing at you. Laughing or talking, it is up to you to listen and figure out what is being said. The following listing of various traditional sounds and noises a bike emits should prove helpful to you. Please be aware however, that bikes are an ornery lot and will come up with new and different noises for the same maladies just to throw you off track. Welcome to finicky mountain bikes.

Thwippity-Thwippity-Thwippity: Your bike has just eaten a small bush, a small mammal, or part of your

YEARGGGGRUMPHEEEOW!!

leg and is flicking the left-overs around in the rear wheel. Dismount and burp the bike.

Hissssssssssssssss: Your bike has a leak somewhere in one of its tires that will take you several hours to find and several days to repair. It is easier to install a new tire. If it is not a leak, then another possibility is that your bike is jeering you after a particularly cowardly move. Beat it over the headset with a rock or heavy log.

Thwackity-Thawarak-Screech: Your bike has just attempted to install a large branch in the rear wheel. The attempt has failed and all the spokes have been ripped from the rim. You now have 3 milliseconds to find a suitable, and hopefully comfortable landing site.

Schlooopscreeeeeeeeeeeeee: Your bike has just used its front brake to grab a branch or other stray material, jamming whatever it is between the brake pad and the front rim. You now have 50% or less braking power and your downhill speed is increasing geometrically— enjoy the ride.

Yeargggrumpheeeowww: While trying to extract your feet from the tight grip of your bike's toeclips you look up in time to enjoy a head-first plunge into a dense bush with thorns.

Thud: You have just directed your head into a low-hanging branch. Prepare to pass out.

What To Do With Leftover Parts

There is a reliable axiom for all amateur bike repair people; you will usually have several, if not more, unknown leftover parts lying around after effecting a home repair. While this can be somewhat disconcerting, especially if you were working on your brakes, it is not cause to completely tear apart your bike searching for an appropriate place for those parts. After all, they may in fact be extras; who knows? However, just to be on the safe side, I would recommend packing them up carefully in a zip-lock baggie, label them (leftover brake parts, or whatever), and carry them with you in your seat or handlebar bag.

Why? Simple. Picture yourself heading towards a very steep drop off with a sudden turn requiring hard braking to slow your speed enough to make the turn. You hear a "ploink-snip-pop" and your brake cable flies off. You plunge off the steep drop screaming and land in a pile at the bottom. Despite the pain, you now can be sure that you know where those spare parts went and should be able to successfully complete the repair, providing you can still move and brought the leftover parts with you. That's what is known as good planning.

Simple Rules For Impossibly Complex Repairs

You won't find this in any repair manual, but when the going gets tough, grab the biggest mallet you can lay your hands on and whap away. Unless the part is unusually delicate, such as a derailleur, you should either be able to scare the part into submission or build up well defined biceps that will look good at beach parties. If the part is unusually delicate, this technique will only serve to hopelessly scatter numerous small parts of your bike all over the garage, but then again, you're not any worse off now than before when you couldn't fix the bike. Just load all the miscellaneous pieces in a bucket, carry them to the bike shop, pour all the parts out on the counter, and make up some story about a spectacular crash and how you lived. The mechanics will be in awe.

General Repair Guidelines

1. Every bike contains approximately 10,000 miniature ball bearings. I say approximately, because no one actually knows. The reason for this uncertainty is that whenever a bike is dismantled, a number of the ball bearings initiate a complex escape plan never to be heard from again. Even in a careful and controlled laboratory test within sterile and sealed rooms, the little buggers managed to get loose. It is rumored the military has secretly hired some of the escapees to instruct troops in POW escape plans, but that rumor cannot be substantiated.

2. Using a bike repair manual will help with the repair just about as much as asking Dan Quayle for advice regarding foreign policy. When in doubt, guess and hammer away.

3. When estimating length of time required for a simple repair, consult astrology charts, navigational charts, square root charts, and add 49 hours.

4. When estimating the cost of a simple repair, call the bike shop and ask for an estimate if their bike mechanic fixed it for you. Then add the original cost of your bike, the cost of the spare parts, the cost of extra spare parts to replace those that you might damage or lose during the home repair, and add the cost of having the bike mechanic undo everything you have done and you should have the approximate cost of performing the repair at home.

6 Touring Or How To Go Where No Sane Person Would Think of Going

Being Prepared

Mountain bike touring is a wonderful way to see the more remote areas of our country and also major thoroughfares of other nations that look remarkably similar to our more remote areas. Dirt roads of the earth are but mere dusty paths to worlds of wonder, discovery, and military checkpoints.

As with any venture, your comfort and success will be directly proportional to the amount of good planning and remaining balance on your credit card.

Being prepared for anything is the Boy Scout creed, and is wisely adopted by any sage traveler, hiker, or mountain biker. Unfortunately, being prepared for anything usually means lugging an inordinate amount of gear strapped to every available exposed part of your bike and anatomy. This is why most bicycle tour companies now have sag wagons. They are named for the original Donner Pass Bicycle Tour

Group whose bikes sagged under the immense weight of preparation and left the hapless party to fend for themselves at the Lake Tahoe Marriott Casino. They lost everything and now live a life of destitution.

Sag wagons are wonderful. They follow faithfully behind carrying all the heavy gear, picking up bikers that suddenly decide pedaling is passe, zoom ahead to set up camp and prepare drinks with little umbrellas for the tired tour. Why bike shops don't sell Sag Wagons as recommended accessories is beyond me.

Of course, who could afford one after properly outfitting yourself for an overnight mountain bike tour. Sure, the tour itself is fairly low cost, sometimes free. It had better be after spending $1,000 on a bike, $2,000 on designer panniers for the bike, $5,000 for camping gear (tent, stove, sleeping bag), and $2,999.99 for freeze dried imitation food, colored and flavored to look approximately like the real thing.

Required Touring Equipment

Your Bike: It should have gears, brakes, frame, seat, pedals, chain, pannier rack, panniers, handlebar bag, seat bag, bike bag, optional vomit bag, optional body bag, and an optional brown bag. If you are planning on riding through a major city at any time, throw in a cute little handlebar-mounted bell for good measure.

Camping Gear: Your stove should be small, compact, and in theory have an adjustable flame. Any experienced camper will tell you that in actual practice, camping stoves put out a flame capable of welding iron piping and have a wide range of adjustments from high to nuclear melt-down. Manufacturers of these stoves suggest they will boil water in three to five minutes, but no one besides a rocket scientist has been able to achieve anything more than tepid water in under ten minutes. If you are lucky enough to reach boiling point there is a little known law of nature, discovered by Isaac Newton's distant cousin, Fig, you should be aware of. When camping, water will cool from boiling to freezing in the same amount of time it takes to pour the water from the cook pot to the awaiting cup.

Camping gear should be rounded out by a compact tent that is only slightly larger than your compact sleeping bag. Practice sleeping at home under a twin sized bed with half the space taken up by camping gear and you should be well prepared for the actual experience. Of course, you could attempt to save weight and money by foregoing buying a tent and sleeping under the stars. I tried this once, and although it didn't rain, I couldn't see the stars for the cloud of mosquitoes and gnats that became immensely hungry about the time I tried to go to sleep. I now carry a blood transfusion kit complete with nurse at all times.

Clothing: The rule "if you don't pack it you will need it" especially applies here. Be sure to bring anything and everything in your closet, even if it means riding a tandem with a U-Haul trailer in tow. A jacket, long pants, extra socks, extra jerseys, gloves, hat, and sunglasses are essential. A formal suit, a leisure suit, a plaid suit, and a selection of items to trade with the various natives you may encounter in places like say, Venice Beach or Coney Island are optional, but recommended.

The Ranger Clark Avoidance Guide

There may come a time in your touring career when you run into a Ranger Clark. He is a big man with a big hat, a big belly, a big belt buckle, big boots, a big gun, and a slight prejudice toward mountain bikers. I wish to go on the record here and state that 99% of all the park rangers that I have been fortunate to encounter have been nothing short of courteous, respectful, and a pleasure to meet. However, there do seem to be a few twisted souls lurking out in the

deepest and darkest forests who live to stomp out lycra and the communist sponsored insurgence of mountain bikes into the US of A.

Rather like the tradition of a first ascent, or the first to discover a rare disease, I have taken the liberty, since I have discovered and categorized this phenomena, to name all rangers with an aggressive anti-mountain bike attitude "Ranger Clark's," after the first ranger I encountered one damp afternoon.

My partner had injured himself on a long ride, it was damp and we were exhausted, having overestimated our abilities. The afternoon was disappearing quickly to evening and we still had a long haul to get back to the car, unless we took the "illegal for mountain bikes" connecting trail that would take us directly back to our car. Not wanting to give the wrong idea, we both removed our front wheels, strapped them to our frames, and carried our bikes out, with great difficulty I might add.

My first view of Ranger Clark was one of a belt buckle supporting a belly framed by a gun and a several menacing pouches. I remember thinking that I had seen this man before in several very bad Hollywood movies about the south and small-town law enforcement.

Something about his speech regarding "idiots on mountain bikes . . . no respect for the law . . . even though I prefer horses I own several bikes myself . . . I could arrest you boys (I was thirty at the time) but I'm just going to give you an expensive ticket," washed through my mind like a bad dream. Seems this ranger failed to listen to our story of woe and failed to observe that the mountain bikes were on our shoulders with the front wheels strapped to the frame. Maybe he thought we were stunt bikers out to trash the trail on one wheel to be different?

In the end and after one blistering letter to the district supervisor that had the literary potential to burst into flames any moment, the citation was removed from our record and Ranger Clark advised to mellow out, I hope. But, he's still out there somewhere. Like the headless horseman, he is apt to appear at any time. Of course, if you are doing something illegal, you deserve Ranger Clark. On the other hand, if you are an innocent fledgling, wandering aimlessly through the woods on a "dark and stormy night," be warned—those bikes Ranger Clark owns are actually mounted like trophies in his game room, with florescent-neon lycra-clad bikers still clutching the handlebars in desperate shock.

On Getting Lost

Getting lost can be a lot of fun, zooming through woods, over hills, and through dales; however, the realization that one is lost is no fun at all. Quite often, upon the realization that one is lost, the first instinct is to execute a carefully planned FOPP. FOPP stands for Full On Pedaling Panic and results in the lost cyclist caroming off trees, logs, rocks and even wildlife in a desperate attempt to find home at a high rate of speed. It is a false notion however, that speed will do anything towards helping a lost cyclist become found.

If you should find yourself lost, the correct procedure is to relax, breath deeply and steadily, and then, realizing your feet are still firmly strapped into the toe-clips, desperately attempt to prevent gravity from dumping you in the inevitable thorn bush nearby.

After untangling yourself from your bike, find the emergency stash of matches you have stored in your panniers for such an occasion and light a rip-roaring good bonfire. The fire is not to keep you warm, but rather to attract the attention of 3,000 firefighters that always appear out of nowhere when a fire is spotted in the forests they protect. Once the firefighters have arrived, ask directions and head for home.

Should a fire be out of the question then resort to vandalism or riding on an illegal trail. This technique is a desperate measure however, because you risk incurring the wrath of Ranger Clark who has an uncanny knack for appearing in the most remote and removed of locations.

Guidebooks

Guidebooks serve two purposes: one is to provide basic information that might be too much trouble for you to find out yourself, like asking directions; the other is to provide fire-starting material in an emergency, such as getting lost after following the now out-of-date directions the guidebook provided.

The following is a list of some of my favorite guidebooks and areas to travel:

Three Seconds Down Half-Dome, Yosemite
East LA After Midnight
To the Top of the World Trade Center and Back
Before the Blast, the Mt. Saint Helens Tour Group Relived
Drunk and Riding Slap-Happy, the Napa Wine Country Tour.

7 Preventing Injuries, Gluing Yourself Back Together, and Personal Bumps and Bruises

Physical Fitness

In order to prevent injuries, a mountain biker must maintain a healthy attitude, a well conditioned body, and a good diet plan. The healthy attitude comes from staying keenly aware of your mortality. Rocks, trees, and concrete walls hurt on impact, avoid them at all costs. A well conditioned body is assured by maintaining a rigid massage schedule with a masseuse that uses oils with extra conditioning agents. This leaves diet.

Be sure your eating habits are nothing short of meticulous. You must gauge every calorie and kilocalorie that enters and leaves your body; well, at least those entering. Stay away from granola at all costs. Granola is bird food which contains high amounts of dried cardboard and wood pulps. A balanced diet consists of equal amounts of chocolate frosted donuts followed by equal amounts of black coffee. Chase this down with either an Italian,

Mexican, or French plate for lunch and several scoops of fudge ripple for dinner. Chinese food and salads are worthless because they leave you bloated for one hour and ravenously hungry the rest of the night. Avoid them at all costs.

One last word of advice regarding diet, everything you eat you sweat. In other words, that pastrami, garlic and onion sandwich you munched one hour ago will become one with your underarms and jersey the rest of the afternoon. Friends or sandwich, it's your choice.

Road Rash

This injury is evidenced by a 300 foot long skid mark on the road or dirt covered by every available layer of skin,

ground side of the unfortunate rider who managed to lay his/her bike down. There is not much one can do about road rash so learn to milk the injury for all the sympathy points you can. Some riders will even go so far as to wear clothing with a hole strategically torn at the hip level revealing the biker's red badge of courage. This will inevitably spark interest from the opposite sex and a question like "Wow, what happened to you?" This is the biker's cue to exaggerate as much as possible, creating an image of the crash that is nothing short of legendary and amazing. It is perfectly acceptable to stretch the truth in this situation, but be careful of giving the impression that you single-handedly overcame world hunger, housed the homeless, and prevented war in the Middle East while crashing your bike; that may be perceived as bragging and is not in good taste.

Uphill Agony

Many people mountain bike for their mental and physical well being. This is why one has to wonder about those that insist on climbing hills like a lycra endowed demon. This is also why one has to wonder about these same demons who are left looking for lung and knee replacements after every ride while those of us who walk and crawl up every hill continue to grin in good health.

Fear

Fear is a given in mountain biking, from the moment a rider leaves the protected confines of his or her driveway. Many cyclists are able to deal with fear by blacking out only momentarily upon seeing an image of twisted metal tubing around flesh and broken bones as they flash by a tree that appears to be moving towards them.

For some, however, fear is a nasty malady. The resulting panic-induced slobbering on one's lycra followed by incessant babbling about a boulder that wouldn't get out of the way is a classic symptom of uncontrolled fear. The only first aid for this person is to load them onto your pannier rack and truck them home to plenty of bed rest and Shirley Temple repeats. After several weeks, they should be ready to try riding around the house on a Big Wheel again. Before long, with lots of love, the affected person will actually be ready to head out on a real bike once more.

Surgically Removing An Implanted Bike

After truly amazing wipe-outs involving lots of dust, flying twisted metal and flesh, the result is usually a pile of impossibly intertwined bike parts and human limbs. If possible, try to lift the entire mess upright onto its wheels and roll it to the nearest emergency room.

If, however, the wheels are not useable, you are faced with a crucial decision. Is this art? If it is indeed an art form, take careful photographs from all angles to ensure preserving the image of rider and bike becoming one forever. Once careful documentation of the art-form has been assured, proceed to unwind all human parts from the bike.

If the pile is not deemed art, then begin separating human and bike parts taking care not to damage the bike any more than is necessary. The reason for protecting the bike, is that riders have been known to sue over irreparable bike damage from negligence during a bike rescue.

Injuries From Bright Lycra

Bright lycra is, of itself, not directly hazardous. However, it does draw immediate attention and that can be truly disastrous. Hot pink and cobalt lycra on a woman with ideal body structure has been known to cause whiplash, head-on

collisions, and face-plants into nearby trees in nearly 100% of all males within a three mile radius of that woman. Those few that survive the initial visual onslaught of neon beauty inevitably fail to withstand the icy stare or well placed elbow of an accompanying spouse. Lest this seems sexist, the same applies for bright purple and fuchsia lycra on well defined thighs and, well, you get the picture—female bikers scattered for miles littering the trail in blinded confusion.

The only practical solution is to wear very dark glasses at all times. It's either that or put up with the pain and agony of having to look at form-fitting lycra and risk an injury inducing crash—that's what I thought, I'd take the risk of crashing too.

8 Citizen Racing - How to Destroy Ego, Body, and Bike While Surrounded by Friends

Observed Trials Riding

This is an area of competition where scoring is similar to that of golf. The rider with the lowest score wins. The course must be ridden and obstacles successfully negotiated without the bike coming to a complete stop or the rider's feet touching the ground. They don't say anything about the head, but I have yet to see anyone try a successful head pivot to an upright riding position. The course itself is a nightmare of obstacles which no sane person would ordinarily attempt, but since everyone is watching, what the hell. The promoter of trials riding is usually a very sick and warped individual who insists that everyone should be able to ride over anything he puts in the way, including a car. Often, promoters have to sneak out of town after the race to avoid being tarred and feathered by competitors who didn't think that riding off a 70 foot wall into a 30 foot deep vat of mud was very funny.

Trials riding is great for spectators however. Where else can you sit in a chair, drink a cold soda, and watch lycra-clad idiots pay $50 for the privilege of destroying their $10,000 bike on a $3 boulder just to say they rode over it without touching their feet to the ground. And they say America isn't great!

Uphill Riding

In this particular competition, riders pit their thighs, lungs, and arms against steep, often loose and muddy terrain to prove who can ride either the furthest or fastest uphill. It is not uncommon for contestants in this highly exciting race (bikes sometimes reach a top speed of three miles per hour) to actively solicit heart, lung, and knee transplants after each event just to stay alive.

Why would anyone want to race uphill? There is really no sane answer to this question. Psychologist Gurt Freewheel feels that the desire to compete in uphill racing stems from an unfulfilled desire to be a professional football player or a divorce lawyer. He is presently seeking a $100,000 grant which he will use to research his theory just as soon as football season is over and his divorce is final.

Stage Races

Stage races are short or long lap-style courses over dirt roads, single track trails, and into the valley of hell itself. Remember, you are doing this because it is fun. It is important to keep telling yourself how much fun you are having as you are performing a slow-motion flip over the handlebars for the crowd, or as you are knee deep in mud, hauling your bike after you with only 30 more miles to go. Yep, sure is fun! Of course, the flip-side is the stories you will have to tell.

When signing the liability release form, there is fine print at the bottom which states clearly that "any racer who

survives this course is allowed a margin of exaggeration and dramatization to a factor of ten in order that his or her feat may become legendary in the minds of friends and acquaintances."

The reason that you are able to successfully exaggerate your racing prowess is that no one was anywhere near the course to watch and verify. Why? Because who wants to hike in over mud and dirt to spend 5 hours swatting mosquitoes and gnats just to watch a 3 second blur whizz by periodically and splatter you with mud?

Downhill Mountain Biking Is For Idiots

The idea of this brilliant event is to get down a particularly steep course, often set up on the advanced slope of a downhill ski resort, faster than anyone else. In order to be scored, the rider and the bike must cross the finish line at the same time. Just as in downhill skiing, spectators crowd the edges of the course to watch, no not the racing, the crashing. And there is lots of it. It is entirely possible that the mogul you are skiing over this winter was an unfortunate downhill mountain biker that became one with the course and was unable to be extracted before the first snow.

A Word Of Caution

Remember that at this stage you are merely mortal. You are warned that as soon as you begin racing, you are treading dangerously close to the fringes of tight fluorescent lycra and neon paint. As long as you can continue to justify racing because you merely want the shirt, all will continue as normal. However, if you begin to enjoy the pain, look forward to steep downhills and raw speed, and begin toying with ways to improve your performance, you will have crossed the fringe of sanity never to return. You will feel an uncontrollable desire to sell your children, sell the house, sell your wife and take up a life of expensive bikes, fast pedaling women, and sleazy motels. At this time, there are no established government programs to help addicted citizen-racers overcome their attraction to pain and neon, but it is hoped, with private funding, that we can help a few unfortunate souls return to a life of family and friends.

Is It Really Worth The Shirt?

In many circles, yes! Although it hurt like hell to get it, and each week you wonder again, in the middle of the course, why you are doing this, you will continue to enter races. Why? Because the gratification of being able to wear the shirt and gain instant recognition by peers like "Wow, you raced in that? How was it?," is worth all the sweat and tears, until the next race anyway. So what if each shirt that is only valued at $8.00 actually cost a $50 entry fee plus $10 in after race beers. It's the notoriety that counts, isn't it?

The Merely Mortal Training Schedule

The following is given as a guide to help you minimize the opportunity for throwing a muscle or pulling an unrecognized body part while in pursuit of that t-shirt:

Monday—Think about riding on Tuesday. Eat and drink heavily. Have a Rolaids.

Tuesday—Realize that this is Tuesday and you should probably ride. Head out of the driveway and to the hills. On the way, stop at a donut shop and consume half-a-dozen chocolate frosted followed by a caffeine chaser. Look at the watch and realize you had better get home before you are late for work.

Wednesday—Go for a ride around the block with some friends that have no neon or tight lycra tendencies.

Thursday—Give your bike a massage.

Friday—Get a massage. Head to the best Italian restaurant you know and consume large amounts of pasta, pastry, and beer in the name of carbo-loading.

Saturday—Go for a ride on actual dirt to get the feel for it.

Sunday—Relax, watch football, basketball, hockey, or nap. Above all, don't allow yourself to be strained by having to clean the house or do yard work. This could throw off your race-day performance. Your spouse will understand.

Emotional Impact Of A Crash

Humor is a very individual thing and is entirely dependent on perspective. What is funny to one is a disaster to another. This is why crashes during a race full of spectators have the potential to be humiliating and have a lasting emotional impact.

When I was fifteen, I was performing a series of stunts on my Schwinn Balloon-Tire-Mobile for an admiring audience of young women—very similar to an observed trials event today. After a particularly difficult top-tube-balance-one-foot-pivot-maneuver I returned to my seat, soaked up the applause and came to an abrupt, face-first stop into a tether-ball pole. I regained consciousness after only a moment with laughter ringing in my ears. "Do that again, you're killing us ha, ha, ha."

In order to help others minimize the emotional impact of stupid crashes in front of large crowds, I have devised the following technique which seems to work well. If you should inadvertently lose control of your bike performing an easy maneuver, make the crash look as serious as possible. Roll, bounce, spin, cartwheel for at least 300 yards. Be sure to begin dismantling your bike during this so that various parts will scatter adding to the imagery of total disaster. The crowd's laughter will turn to horror. I even carry a plastic arm (looks real) in my bike bag that I toss for added effect if needed. Lie very still after the dust settles and let the ambulance people cart you off. After about five minutes, slip the paramedic a $50 and walk (limp if you can fake it well enough) out of the ambulance to the adoring applause of the crowd. You have just turned potential embarrassment into glorified adoration. So much for emotional impact.

Drafting

While most cyclists will tell you drafting means to ride close enough behind another rider so you get caught up in his draft thereby reducing wind resistance, in mountain biking this is a mute point. No one goes fast enough to get caught up in anyone's draft, except if someone sneezes.

The approved and accepted way of drafting in mountain biking requires consuming 10 to 13 draft beers, in rapid succession, before the race. This way, the mountain biker is so relaxed that even the worst crash or worst hill climb fades into fuzzy recollection as the reality of a first class hangover kicks in.

9

The Mountain Bike Survivalist's Dictionary of Necessary and Ridiculous Terminology

Apres-ride Gathering: The gathering of riders at a bar after a race or ride to replenish bodily fluids and engage in animated discussions that offer 30-minute detailed descriptions of crashes and special moments that took all of 2 seconds to occur. Also an opportunity for riders to offer new and unique reasons for poor performance and failed moves.

Bike Hiking: A little recognized recreational activity enjoyed by millions of people every year (less so now than when an all-terrain bike weighed 10 tons). To bike hike properly, one must find a suitable trail with an incline gradient similar to that of a vertical wall and then hike up it pushing or dragging the bike along. Friends tell me that all the effort is well worth it just for the downhill ride, but my bike and I have yet to enjoy that experience at the same time so I really couldn't comment except to say that I have heard it is so.

Chainring: The set of multi-toothed rings attached to the pedal that grab the chain to provide forward momentum to a biking experience. Also, the multi-toothed rings that grab loose articles of clothing, such as a pant leg, and have an appetite for flesh when a rider separates from his bike during a momentum-enhancing downhill plunge.

Clean: As in "cleaned the monster log." Means to successfully negotiate something on a bike that is so difficult no one in their right mind would attempt and those that attempted it before had to be cleaned off the log themselves.

Endo: An elegant over the handlebar swan dive resulting from too much front brake, too much body weight forward, and too much downhill angle which results in too much pain for too little pleasure.

Fat Tires: Overweight tires with a remarkable gift for providing just enough traction to allow mountain bikers a moment of glory before washing out and dumping cyclist and cycle in an inseparable heap. The only part of the bike or cyclist that will not be permanently damaged after getting dumped.

Front End Washout: An unpleasant situation that sometimes occurs to one rider (usually male) who, while clutching a beer with one hand after a great day of riding, makes an off-color comment about sexual prowess that leaves everyone (including members of the opposite sex) doubled up hysterically. Also refers to the sickening feeling that precedes a complete loss of control as the rider realizes that the front end of the bike is heading in an unintended direction at a high rate of speed.

Guidebook: A carefully researched and written book complete with detailed maps and trail descriptions that would have proved immensely helpful on today's ride except for the fact that it is still sitting on the bookshelf at home.

High Cadence Spinning: The act of pedaling fifty times faster than the rate of visible forward momentum leaving the cyclist exhausted and the bike heading nowhere fast.

Honk Your Brains Out: The act of climbing a steep hill with great power for an extended period of time leaving the cyclist breathing so hard that the brains "get honked out" through the nose and onto the trail. Also refers to an extreme sneeze or a violent blowing of the nose in an attempt to expel a massive build-up of dust.

Mountain Bike Racing: An event dreamed up by a sadist who enjoys watching several thousand cyclists disappear in a cloud of dust as they all madly bob and weave their way to one massive entanglement that even a Rubic's Cube master would have trouble freeing.

Off Camber: Any trail surface that heads into a turn leaning in the direction of the turn, leaving the rider sliding out of the turn and wishing his luck hadn't take a turn for the worse.

Off Roading: Any form of bicycling that results in the rider (and bike) voluntarily (or unexpectedly) leaving a paved environment for dirt, mud, and pain.

On Your Left!: Or on your right! is a warning often screamed by a downhill cyclist approaching another cyclist or hiker at a high rate of speed from behind, which results in startling that person so much that they move in the direction that was screamed causing a spectacular crash.

Performance Riding Position: Any position a rider assumes that is somewhat on the bike while the bike is barreling down a hill at an impossible rate of descent.

Quick Release: This feature on most bikes today allows the rider to quickly remove his wheel in the event of a flat without having to use tools. This nifty design feature also allows the wheel to quickly remove itself from the bike if the bike owner fails to tighten the lever which leaves the bike owner being quickly released from the bike and quickly admitted to the emergency room.

Shock Absorption: The feeling of numbness that envelops one's posterior after several hours of riding on a particularly rocky path while sitting on a ergonomically designed bike seat that was never intended to be ridden by humans.

Single Track: An extremely narrow and steep route that is barely wide enough for someone to hike on, let alone pedal. The difficulty of single track riding is found in the realization that should the rider lose control, he has nowhere to turn except into extreme dense foliage (poison oak), extremely dense rock (a rock wall), or extreme open space (off a cliff).

Skid Turn: A 180 degree power turn that leaves anyone within 50 feet showered with dirt and choking in dust. One power turn can uproot an entire forest. Also a technique often attempted after a race by contestants to impress friends, but usually resulting in the contestant losing control and "spiking" himself in front of his friends, which at least provides for their amusement if not his.

Skinny Tires: Any tire that has enrolled in a Jenny Craig weight loss program. Useless for riding off-road.

Technical Terrain: A given bike route considered in terms of steepness, irregularity of surface, narrowness of trail, sharpness of turns, presence of large unavoidable obstacles, and the likelihood of pain and fear while riding it.

Top Tube: The section of a bike frame designed to add strength to the bicycle and provide a resting place for the groin should the cyclist happen to inadvertently leave his seat during a ride.

Unweighting: A quick compression of the front tire followed by an immediate jumping and lifting using the handlebar and toeclips. This results in the bike "bunny hopping" over ruts and other obstacles and ends up with the rider clinging to the bike in panic as it continues to hippity hop down the rest of the hill.

Urban Cycling: Any cycling that is not on dirt and is accompanied by buses, pedestrians, rude gestures, broken glass and railroad tracks.

White Knuckle Factor: The way in which many ardent riders and some bicycle magazine reviewers refer to the difficulty of terrain. A white-knuckle factor of ten means complete panic and often requires surgery to remove the cyclist's hands from the handlebars.

Mountain Biking For Mere Mortals Index